D1090662

CHOMP!

THE GREAT WHITE SHARK
AND OTHER ANIMALS THAT BITE

Greg Roza

PowerKiDS
press
New York

Published in 2011 by The Rosen Publishing Group, Inc.
29 East 21st Street, New York, NY 10010

First Edition

Editor: Jennifer Way
Book Design: Kate Laczynski

Photo Credits: Cover, pp. 1, 6, 7 (top), 8, 9, 17 (top), 19, 20–21 Shutterstock.com; p. 4 David Fleetham/Visuals Unlimited, Inc./Getty Images; p. 5 © Tom Brakefield/Stockbyte/Thinkstock; pp. 7 (bottom), 12 © iStockphoto/Thinkstock; p. 10 © www.iStockphoto.com/Chris Dascher; p. 11 (top) Ian Waldie/Getty Images; p. 11 (bottom) Mike Parry/Getty Images; p. 13 © Chris and Monique Fallows/Peter Arnold, Inc.; p. 14 © www.iStockphoto.com/Andy Gehrig; p. 15 Nick Norman/Getty Images; p. 16 © www.iStockphoto.com/René Lorenz; p. 17 (bottom) Martin Harvey/Getty Images; p. 18 Paul A. Zahl/Getty Images; p. 22 Cyril Ruoso/JH Editorial/Getty Images.

Library of Congress Cataloging-in-Publication Data

Roza, Greg.
  Chomp! : the great white shark and other animals that bite / by Greg Roza. — 1st ed.
      p. cm. — (Armed and dangerous)
Includes index.
ISBN 978-1-4488-2551-6 (library binding) — ISBN 978-1-4488-2686-5 (pbk.) — ISBN 978-1-4488-2687-2 (6-pack)
  1. Dangerous animals—Juvenile literature. 2. White shark—Juvenile literature. I. Title.
QL100.R693 2011
591.6'5—dc22
                                        2010027080

Manufactured in the United States of America

CPSIA Compliance Information: Batch #WW11PK: For Further Information contact Rosen Publishing, New York, New York at 1-800-237-9932

CONTENTS

ANIMAL BITES!

In the wild, sharp teeth are always helpful. Many **predators**, such as the great white shark, use their teeth to catch and tear apart their **prey**. Sometimes all an animal has to do is show their sharp teeth to scare

Great white sharks live in coastal ocean waters throughout much of the world.

another animal away. Other animals use their teeth to **defend** themselves from predators.

In this book, we will take a closer look at some of the world's successful predators and how they hunt with their teeth. We will also meet a few animals that use their teeth to stay safe.

ALL KINDS OF TEETH

Animals have different kinds of teeth based on what they eat. A deer eats plants. It has knifelike front teeth for cutting grass and flat back teeth for grinding food. A lion eats meat. It has sharp **fangs** to hold on to its prey. It also has sharp back teeth that act

The shape of deer's teeth helps them cut and chew plants.

Some snakes can give a venomous bite. You can see the venom dripping down the fangs of the snake shown here.

like scissors to cut meat into small pieces. Lions and deer both use their teeth to defend themselves.

Some animals add **venom** to their bite! Many snakes that have fangs are venomous. Venom can cause pain and swelling, or it can kill.

Lions use their huge, sharp teeth for killing prey.

PREDATOR AND PREY

Most predators have sharp teeth for holding prey and tearing flesh. However, not all animals use their sharp teeth for hunting. The wombat uses its sharp front teeth to **gnaw** plants. It may also use them to give predators a nasty bite! People are warned to stay far away from wombats.

Wombats might not look scary. They are ready to defend themselves with their sharp teeth, though.

The Tasmanian devil, shown here, is one of the wombat's few enemies. Here you can see the Tasmanian devil's sharp teeth.

The Tasmanian devil is one of the wombat's greatest enemies. It has sharp teeth, powerful **jaws**, and one of the strongest bites of any **mammal** in the world! The Tasmanian devil is also daring enough to bite a wombat before a wombat can bite it back.

GREAT WHITE SHARK

Great white sharks are the largest predators in the sea. They can grow to be more than 20 feet (6 m) long and weigh more than 5,000 pounds (2,268 kg).

A great white has about 3,000 razor-sharp teeth! The upper teeth are large and triangular for sawing

Sharks move quickly when they are hunting. While chasing prey, they can reach speeds of more than 25 miles per hour (40 km/h).

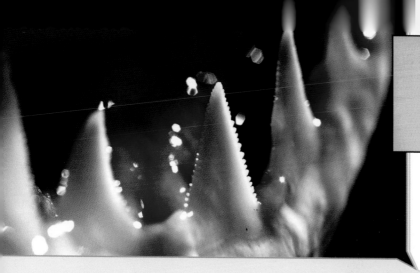

through flesh. The narrow bottom teeth help a great white hold on to its prey. Each jaw has three rows of teeth. When a great white loses a front-row tooth, another moves up to fill in the space. A great white might have as many as 20,000 teeth in its lifetime!

Great white sharks have strong jaw muscles that help their teeth tear into and hold on to prey.

SHARK ATTACK!

Great white sharks are always looking for food. Young great whites eat fish and small sea mammals. Adults hunt seals, sea lions, and small whales. They will also eat dead animals they find.

When a great white **attacks**, it opens its mouth very wide. Then it chomps down, sinking its sharp teeth

This is a sea lion. Sea lions make good meals for great white sharks because their bodies have a lot of fat.

into its prey. As the great white swings its head back and forth, its teeth saw through the prey's flesh and tear it into smaller pieces. Sometimes a great white will bite an animal and then wait for it to bleed to death before eating it.

POLAR BEAR

While the great white shark is the largest hunter in the sea, the polar bear is in the running for that title on land. Polar bears can grow to be up to 10 feet (3 m) long and weigh up to 1,700 pounds (771 kg)!

Polar bears live in the Far North, above the Arctic Circle. Although they are born on land, they spend most of their lives on the sea ice.

Polar bears eat mostly seals, like the ringed seal shown here. The polar bear's white fur helps it blend in with its icy habitat and sneak up on its prey.

Polar bears eat mostly seals, but they will eat just about any animal they can catch. Adult polar bears have 42 teeth. They have three different kinds of teeth. Their knifelike front teeth can tear through animal flesh. Their sharp fangs hold on to prey. Polar bears also have strong back teeth for chewing.

SALTWATER CROCODILE

The saltwater crocodile is the largest **reptile** in the world. Some saltwater crocodiles grow to be up to 23 feet (7 m) long and weigh 1,000 pounds (454 kg). They also have 68 pointy teeth!

The saltwater crocodile is known as a top-level predator. That means adult saltwater crocodiles can kill almost any animal in their habitat and that no other animals hunt them.

Saltwater crocodiles hunt all kinds of land animals, such as kangaroos.

The saltwater crocodile eats just about anything it can catch. It hides in water and waits for an animal to swim by or walk up to the water. The crocodile quickly chomps down on the prey with its powerful jaws. The crocodile's sharp teeth hold on to the prey while it twists and drags the prey under water. Crocodiles will work together to tear larger animals apart.

Saltwater crocodiles can quickly jump out of the water to bite their prey.

17

PIRANHA

The piranha is a fish with powerful jaws and razor-sharp teeth. Piranhas' top and bottom teeth fit together perfectly. This allows the piranha to easily rip hunks of flesh off passing fish. If a piranha loses a tooth, another one will grow in its place.

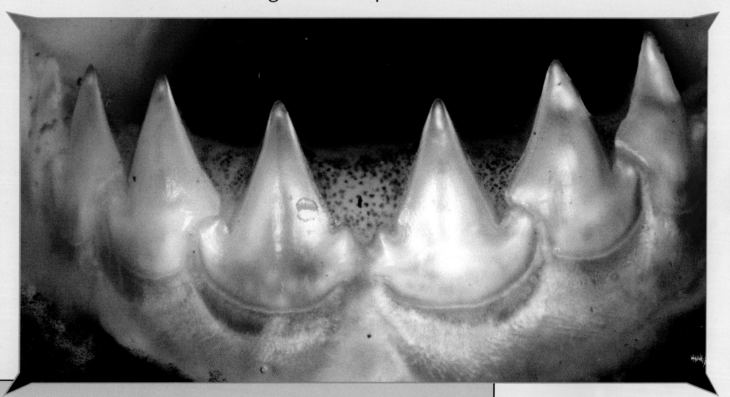

Here is a close-up look at a piranha's teeth. Piranhas live in rivers in South America. They are not large fish. Most are about 6 to 10 inches (15–25 cm) long.

Piranhas are sometimes scavengers. This means that they eat dead or dying animals that they find.

Sometimes piranhas form groups of 20 or more. They form these groups to defend themselves from larger predators. Piranhas sometimes bite people and larger animals swimming in the river. They eat mostly other fish and sometimes other piranhas, too!

FUN FACTS

1 The 1975 movie *Jaws* is about a 25-foot- (8 m) long great white shark. The shark in the movie attacks and eats people. Great whites almost never do this, though.

2 Scientists think great whites do not really like how people taste. In most shark attacks, people are bitten just once, as though the sharks were "tasting" the people before swimming away.

3 Polar bears eat seals. They sit near holes in the ice and wait for seals to come up for air. Then the polar bears grab them with their teeth or claws!

If a saltwater crocodile loses a tooth, another one will grow in its place.

You can tell a crocodile from an alligator by looking at its teeth. Crocodiles have two bottom teeth that stick out when their mouths are closed, and alligators do not.

Piranhas have earned a bad name as bloodthirsty killers. However, some people keep them as pets!

STAY AWAY!

Great white shark, polar bear, and piranha attacks on people are pretty uncommon, although they do occur. Crocodiles, however, are not picky eaters. They will try to eat anyone foolish enough to get too close!

Bites from other, smaller animals can be dangerous because animals can pass on illnesses to people when they bite. Many woodland animals can pass on rabies. Rabies is an illness that affects the brain and leads to death if it is not treated quickly. It is a good idea to stay away from wild animals with sharp teeth since most will not be afraid to use them to attack and defend.

GLOSSARY

attacks (uh-TAKS) Charges at.

defend (dih-FEND) To guard from being hurt.

fangs (FANGZ) Long, sharp teeth.

gnaw (NAW) To keep on biting something.

jaws (JAHZ) Bones in the top and bottom of the mouth.

mammal (MA-mul) A warm-blooded animal that has a backbone and hair, breathes air, and feeds milk to its young.

predators (PREH-duh-terz) Animals that kill other animals for food.

prey (PRAY) An animal that is hunted by another animal for food.

reptile (REP-tyl) A cold-blooded animal with thin, dry pieces of skin called scales.

venom (VEH-num) A poison passed by one animal into another through a bite or a sting.

INDEX

WEB SITES

Due to the changing nature of Internet links, PowerKids Press has developed an online list of Web sites related to the subject of this book. This site is updated regularly. Please use this link to access the list:
www.powerkidslinks.com/armd/chomp/